WORSHIP QUEST:
A Biblical Exploration
of Worship & Music

featuring the song

"More Than You Think I Am"

written by Danny Gokey,

Bernie Herms, and Tim Nichols

A Biblical Exploration of Worship & Music

featuring the song

"More Than You Think I Am"

written by Danny Gokey,

Bernie Herms, and Tim Nichols

Christine Young

Perceptions Publishing

Perceptions Publishing
Tawas City, Michigan, USA
www.worshipquest.com
Printed in the U.S.A.

Worship Quest: A Biblical Exploration of Worship & Music "More Than You Think I Am"
Copyright 2021 by Christine Young

This edition: ISBN 978-1-7365450-0-3

This title is available at Amazon (KDP). Updated sales locations are listed on the Worship Quest website, www.worshipquest.com.

Requests for information, training and event bookings should be addressed to:
Perceptions Publishing, 136 Oates Rd., Tawas City, Michigan 48763

First printing January 2021/Printed in the United States of America

Contents

Essential Resources @ www.worshipquest.com

   ♀ Weekly Teaching Videos

   ♀ Leader Guide

   ♀ Finale Celebration Planning Guide

   ♀ Meditation Moments: Writing Exercises

How to Use This Guide

Welcome to Worship Quest: A Biblical Exploration of Worship & Music, the first book in the Worship Quest series in which music invites the reader to search out scriptural truth. Our "signature song" provides the framework for further biblical exploration and investigation over a period of 5 to 6 weeks.

You will be challenged to go deeper into the Word, to expand your understanding of who God is and to express worship in various ways. As it states in Psalm 1, we want to be "like a tree firmly planted by streams of water." The "water" is His Holy Word. (Ephesians 5:25-26)

Each weekly session includes a group lesson and five days of personal study time. The exception is in Lesson Six which is intended to be an optional finale celebration of worship, music, art, and wrap-up testimonials.

Each weekly group lesson consists of the following eight components:
- Prelude - introductory connection questions (5-10 minutes)
- Video - short teaching video (15-20 minutes) with listening notes
- Encore - large group discussion (5-10 minutes)
- Overture - listen to signature song selection (5 minutes)
- Lyrics & Lessons - study the song and scriptures (15-20 minutes)
- Application – information to transformation (5-10 minutes)
- Rest - quiet reflection (3-5 minutes)
- Prayer – as time permits

INDEX of commonly used icons and terms

 Small Group
Discussion

 Scripture Study

 Listen

 Leader or Volunteer
Reads Aloud

 Lyrics and Lessons (study the song and scripture)

 Musical symbol for **REST**. Stop and reflect on the Word. In Hebrew it would be *Selah*: pause, rest, silence.

 Social Media icon indicates a suggested portion of the personal study for you to consider posting on your social media sites between group studies.

 Encore means return to stage. In our study, it means we return to a larger group discussion.

Overture means prelude or intro to a greater work. This is when we listen to our featured song choice and start to study it for scriptural content.

Prelude is an action or event serving as an introduction to something more important. In our study, we check in with one another at the beginning of our weekly sessions.

Session 1

OUR QUEST BEGINS

Behold, I will do something new, now it will spring forth; will you not be aware of it? I will even make a roadway in the wilderness, rivers in the desert.

-Isaiah 43:19, New American Standard Bible (NASB)

Lesson One: Our Quest Begins

 Prelude

Small Group – Connection Questions

(*Try to be in groups no larger than 4 or 5. Allot 5-10 minutes.*)

- Introduce yourselves to one another.

- Think of a song that reminds you of an event or specific time period from your life. If one comes to mind, please share.

Video Listening Notes (13 minutes)

The teaching videos are online at www.worshipquest.com, under the Resources tab.

WHAT? *A Worship Quest* is a biblical exploration of worship and music in which we examine the song structure of one song in each *Worship Quest* study for 5 to 6 weeks. This study allows us to break down the lyrics and discover biblical truths and themes that aren't readily apparent as we listen to or sing the song.

The more we know God's truth, the more we will love God and love others.

Our truth intake is relative to our worship output.

The Bible is the inspired Word of God and the only infallible rule of faith and conduct. (2 Timothy 3:16,17)

Although we are utilizing music, it doesn't take precedence over the Holy Scriptures. Music is merely an access point that takes us deeper into the Word and is utilized for the purpose of learning biblical truth.

Word Study: Worship

Worship is central to our entire life purpose.

Every deed, every action that we perform can be done to the glory of God and can serve as worship.

Chris' Definition:

Worship is a verb, an intention of the heart, an action.

Worship is a lifestyle that should extend into every waking moment of our lives.

Word Study: Quest

Merriam-Webster's dictionary states that it is a "jury of inquest, investigation, a pursuit or search. As a verb it means "to search for or to ask for."

Dictionary.com says it is "a search or a pursuit made in order to obtain something."

If you look at the word 'inquest,' we find that its synonyms are inquiry, investigation, probe, review, study, survey, examination, exploration, etc.

We are on a spiritual quest for truth!

HOW?

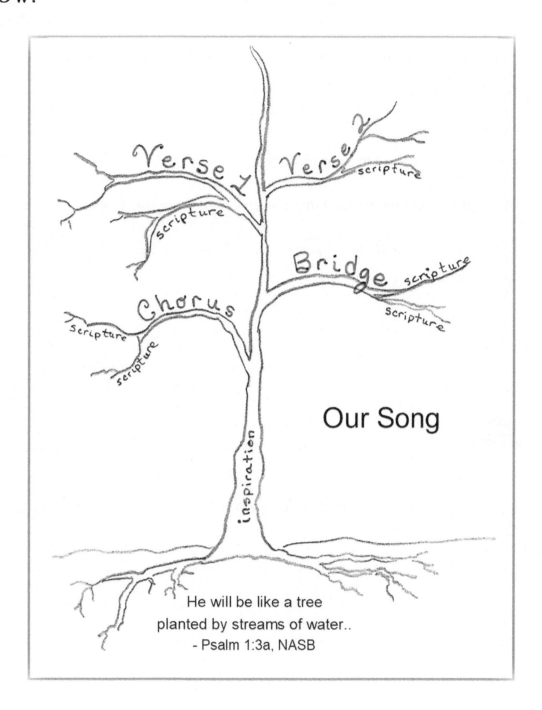

Verse 1 Verse 2 scripture scripture Bridge scripture scripture Chorus scripture scripture Our Song inspiration

He will be like a tree
planted by streams of water..
- Psalm 1:3a, NASB

Psalm 1:2-3 reads "but his delight is in the law of the Lord, and in His law he meditates day and night. *He will be like a tree firmly planted by streams of water*, which yields its fruit in its season and its leaf does not wither; And in whatever he does, he prospers." (NASB, Italics mine)

A chorus is the section of the song that gets repeated over and over. The words do not change.

A verse (aka 'stanza') has the same tune or melody, but the words change.

A bridge is the part of the song that sounds a bit different. It has a different melody (tune) and lyric (words) from any other section.

 Encore
[means *return to stage*. In this case it means start large group discussion ☺]

Q. What stood out to you in the video teaching? Anything new or interesting?

Overture

[means prelude or intro to
a greater work. In this case,
the greater work is our Signature Song]

Listen while reading the words.

Allot 5 minutes.

More Than You Think I Am
Gokey, Herms, Nichols

Verse 1

You always think I'm somewhere on a
mountain top
but never think behind bars
You'd be amazed the places that I'd go,
to be with you,
where you are
So forget what you've heard
what you think that you know
There's a lot about Me
that's never been told

CHORUS

I'm more than you dream
More than you understand
Your days and your times
were destined for our dance
I catch all your tears
Burn your name on My heart
Be still and trust My plan
I'm more than you think I am
More than you think I am

Verse 2

Rumor has it there's a gavel
in My hand
I'm only here to condemn
But let Me tell you secrets you would
never know
I think of you as My best friend
So much has been said
even done in My name
but I'm showing you now
Who I really am

Bridge:

Let Me open your eyes to see the
heart of Me, differently, oh
Let Me in like never before
Bring Me every broken part
the wounds and scars of who you
are and hide in Me and you will see

Reprinted with permission

More than you understand

your days & your times

were destined for our dance

I'm more than you dream

Chorus Part 1

CHORUS
Part One

He will be like a tree
planted by streams of water..
- Psalm 1:3a, NASB

Study the illustration for a moment. Notice how the branches have the lyrics and Scripture references on them. This song is loaded with scripture and has many treasures for us to investigate.

Assign the definitions to participants to read aloud. (Allot 5-10 minutes.) Facilitator: If you break into small groups rather than staying in one large group for this section, return to the larger group for the group questions.

1. The word *worship* comes from the Saxon word *weorthscype*, which later became worthship. To worship God is to ascribe the proper worth to God, to magnify His worthiness of praise, or better, to approach and address God as He is worthy…the more we focus on God, the more we understand and appreciate how worthy He is. As we understand and appreciate this, we can't help but respond to Him. Just as an incredible sunset or breathtaking mountaintop vista evokes a spontaneous response, so we cannot encounter the worthiness of God without the response of *worship*.[1]

   – Dr. Donald Whitney, author and professor

2. *Worship* is the direct acknowledgement to God, of his nature, attributes, ways and claims, whether by the outgoing of the heart in praise and thanksgiving, or by deed done in such acknowledgement.[2] – Vine's Dictionary

3. *Worship* is the ultimate goal of the church; all of history is moving toward one great goal, the white-hot worship of God and his Son among all the peoples of the earth.[3] – Dr. John Piper, author, pastor and theologian

4. To *worship* is to quicken the conscience by the holiness of God; to feed the mind with the truth of God; to purge the imagination by the beauty of God; to open up the heart to the love of God; to devote the will to the purpose of God.[4] – William Temple, former Archbishop of Canterbury

5. True *worship* is defined by the priority we place on *who* God is in our lives and *where* God is on our list of priorities. True worship is a matter of the heart expressed through a lifestyle of holiness.[5] – Rev. Dr. Delesslyn A. Kennebrew, J.D., M. Div., author and minister

Group Questions

Q. For the benefit of the whole group, what stood out to you, on the word "worship?"

Q. Are there any key words or phrases that you should write down for your own personal definition?

Take Notes Here:

We begin our *Worship Quest* by unpacking the chorus, which is always the most repeated portion of any song. Here is the first half of the chorus:

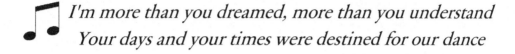
I'm more than you dreamed, more than you understand
Your days and your times were destined for our dance

As we look at this first line of the chorus. It's interesting to note that there are many more verses about dreams and visions in the Old Testament than there are in the New Testament. Why is that? Did dreams or visions occur more before Jesus came? Do people dream as much today as they did back then? Of course, we're not going to solve that mystery today. What we do know is that in the Old Testament Jesus (the Holy Spirit) had not yet come, so dreams and visions were a common way for God to communicate to His people.

	Bible	Old Testament	New Testament
verses with "dream"	93	85	8
verses with "vision"	121	99	22

Source: www.biblegateway.com

** See website for step-by-step word study instructions

Back to the song lyric. The "I" in the lyric represents God saying that He is more than we can dream and more than we can understand. We cannot dream bigger dreams than God dreams for us and we cannot fully comprehend, or understand, everything about God.

 Read Ephesians 3:14-21
{Pro Tip – access different versions on your phone}

Fill in the blanks from verse 20 from the New American Standard Bible (NASB):

Now to _____ who is able to do _____ _____ _____ beyond all that we ask or_____, according to the power that works within us,

Now read it in New Living Translation *(NLT)* version. Fill in the blanks:

Now all glory to God, who is able, through his mighty power at work within us, to accomplish _____ more than we might ask or think.

Q. Based on that scripture, how do you think your abilities or thoughts compare with God's?

Read Isaiah 55:8,9 (This author prefers the New American Standard Bible version, known as NASB. Use whichever version you prefer.)

Q. Based on that scripture, how do you our abilities or thoughts compare with God's?

 WRITE OUT Psalm 139:16. Try to use up the space allotted. Maybe make one word bigger than the others.

 Read Psalm 90:12

Q. What can we know about our "days" from these verses?

Q. What do you think is meant by "numbering our days" and in what practical ways can you do that?

It is an excellent art rightly to **number our days**, so as not to be out in our calculation, as he was who counted upon many years to come when, that night, his soul was required of him. We must live under a constant apprehension of the shortness and uncertainty of life and the near approach of death and eternity. We must so number our days as to compare our work with them, and mind it accordingly with a double diligence, as those that have no time to trifle. [6]

 Application: Making the Lesson Practical

Discuss as a group or take home if time doesn't allow for that. If you are in multiple small groups, move to a full group discussion.

What action steps can we list from the information that we have just studied? Participants take a few minutes to look back over the lesson and find action steps that you can share with the group. Group leader, record ideas on a whiteboard if possible. Participants, write the shared responses here:

Here are a few examples:

- ☼ Remember that worship is a lifestyle that should extend into every waking moment of your life. That is my short definition. What is yours?

- ☼ Remember that "worship is defined by the priority we place on who God is in our lives and where God is on our list of priorities." (Kennebrew) Where is God on your list of priorities? How do you or can you include Him in your day?

Other Action Steps:

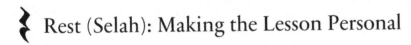

⸮ Rest (Selah): Making the Lesson Personal

This symbol means "rest." Take a moment now to be quiet. (3-5 minutes)

Selah is a word used 74 times in the Hebrew Bible (Old Testament)—seventy-one times in the Psalms and three times in the Book of Habakkuk.

Although the exact meaning of the word is a mystery, "Based on the content, it is generally accepted that Selah is a musical term of some sort and is there to provide musical direction…many commentators think that Selah meant 'to pause' or 'to reflect'. This could have been a request for the reader or listener to pause and think about what has been said, or it could have been a space for voices to pause and for instruments to play alone." [7]

Review the pages that you have just worked on today. Here are some questions that you might consider during this quiet time:

- ☿ What is God telling you to do about how your days are spent? Write it out and date it.

- ☿ What is the one thing that stood out to you that you want to remember?

- ☿ Is there anything that you want to study further?

- ☿ What might God be impressing on you today?

Record your thoughts here:

Review the definitions of worship (pages 17 & 18) and begin to write down your own personal definition of worship, or key words for worship that stood out to you today.

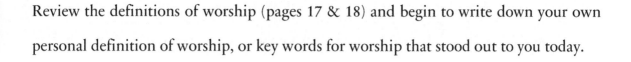

Prayer

Close out this session by praying for one another in large or small groups. Use your *Prayer Pages* in the back of this book to share, record and remember prayer requests.

Rejoice always; pray without ceasing; in everything give thanks; for this is God's will for you in Christ Jesus. - 1 Thessalonians 5:16-18 (NASB)

Personal Study: Going Deeper, Day by Day

You have just studied scripture about how valuable your days are. Your personal study time is designed to let you not only dive deeper but also to linger and soak in God's Word. Let it become a part of you. Make time for it.

I have done so many Bible studies that I have really loved, and then weeks later I could barely recall the title, let alone the content. I strongly believe that we need to spend more time and meditate on the truth until it sinks in. We can't just gloss over it. We are taking in so much information every day and not soaking in the Word. Like drinking water, we need to be satiated and completely hydrated. Daily.

For this reason, your daily time with God is structured to be both a review of what was covered in class and a development of the ideas that were touched on.

I've also made a point to purposely not put the text for all the scriptures into this study guide. I love it when authors put the scripture right in view, but I find that I get lazy about looking up scripture in an actual Bible. I'm spoon-fed, and I like it, but I'm not growing up as much as I would if I were to find the scriptures on my own. You'll notice that I ask you to write out scriptures often and that is to your benefit ☺. These holy habits will help you slow down and soak in the Word. You can also visit the website for more writing examples.

Ways to Go Deeper:

- Write out scripture (either the whole verse, part of the verse, or one word) and/or try a word lettering technique from the back of this book on page 141. You can also upload your work to inspire others to do the same at www.worshipquest.com

- Make yourself an index card or take a picture on your phone so you can think about a key verse or idea throughout the week. Remember that writing scripture out (rather than just taking a picture of it) helps you retain the Word. It's neuroscience!

- Tape your index card or paper with a scripture verse or word on it into your book or day planner. Washi tape works great and can put taken off and on easily.

- Listen to the signature song (More Than You Think I Am) throughout the week.

- Participate in any Social Media activity (listed in your lesson) if your leader chooses to do so.

- Connect with someone else in your study group throughout the week to discuss your thoughts and possibly participate in word exercises together. Meet at a coffee shop?

- Review the information (the application section in particular).

Day One – Worship

Go back and review the definitions of worship (pages 17 and 18). What stood out to you or what did you learn or relearn from those definitions?

Q. Which definition is your favorite one? Why?

Q. What key words or ideas appeal to you?

Spend some time reviewing what you've studied and learned about worship so far, and *then write out your own definition of worship.* Your definition will be a work in progress over the next few weeks as we learn more about worship, so don't stress about this task!

Write down what you think worship means to you, in your own words. Consider these sentence starters as you work out your own definition.

- The words that come to mind when I think of worship are...
- To worship something or someone, I would...
- To worship God means to...

☼ There is plenty of space on this page for your personal definition of worship, which should inspire you to revisit this item repeatedly over the next several weeks to refine and expand your definition. ☺

This week's OPTIONAL SOCIAL MEDIA ITEM:

(if applicable, ask group leader)

 If time allows, spend a few minutes online (or in other resources) looking for *another definition of worship* that you like. Write it out here and note where you found it (so you can share it in class next week). OR, if you already have one that you appreciate, *write it here and/or post it on your social media site this week.*

Take a moment now to be quiet and think about how you can worship God today. Ask Him to enlarge your understanding of what it means to worship Him, in spirit and in truth, in practical ways.

   ☼   Take time to pray for the requests that you have on your *Prayer Pages* in the back of this book.

Day Two – More Than You Dream or Understand

The chorus lyrics begin with "I'm more than you dream, more than you understand." Do you agree with that statement?

Recently my daughter Emily was home visiting for the weekend, and she told me that we just *had* to watch the musical, "*The Greatest Showman.*" She was over the moon about the songs and the actors. We watched it and she was right. I loved it too. Beautiful artistry, actors, music, etc. I have since bought the DVD because I enjoyed it so much. I especially love the song "A Million Dreams."

Here are the lyrics from the chorus:

> 'Cause every night I lie in bed
> The brightest colors fill my head
> A million dreams are keeping me awake
> I think of what the world could be
> A vision of the one I see
> A million dreams is all it's gonna take
> A million dreams for the world we're gonna make

We can dream "a million dreams" and never come close to the dreams or plans that God has in mind for us. We can learn every scripture and become the most educated person on earth and yet never even come close to comprehending all that God knows. Not even close.

Even so, God created us to dream and imagine. How do I know this? Because He created us in His image, and He is the Greatest Creator of all time. You may think you are not "creative," but you would be mistaken. You were made in His image and likeness. (Genesis 1:27)

Can you think of dreams that you have had for your life that God has fulfilled? Can you think of dreams that God has not fulfilled?

Have there been times in your life when you thought that you "know better;" that if you were in charge, you would have a better way to do things? Who actually knows what is best for you in life?

   ☼ Read Psalm 139. What does that Psalm reveal about God "knowing" you and what's best for you?

✧ Review, meditate, write out Isaiah 55:8 and 9 today.

✧ In what practical ways can you incorporate these scriptures into your life?

✧ Take time to pray for the requests that you have on your *Prayer Pages* in the back of this book.

Day Three – More than You Dream or Understand, continued

In the 1989 movie, "Uncle Buck," there is a scene when Buck gets called in to the elementary school because his niece, Maizy, is in "trouble." I use that word loosely because soon the principal will be the one in trouble. The principal of this sweet 6-year-old student tells Buck that "she is a dreamer and a silly heart. I doubt she takes one thing in her career at this school seriously." And Buck answers back that "I don't want to know a six-year-old who isn't a dreamer or a silly heart."

As we get older our tendency can be to shut our dreams down or not dream as big. That may be because words of doubt were spoken to us or because our own thoughts limit our potential. Reasoning can crowd out our dreaming.

Would you say that God has exceeded the dreams that you have had for yourself? Do you still have dreams that you want to see fulfilled? If so, what are they?

If you were on a path toward your dream and it was diverted into another direction, it was for your good and God's glory (Romans 8:28). That can be a tough pill to swallow, right? Can you accept that truth?

Can you accept the truth that God is able to do more than you can dream or think, as scripture says in Ephesians 3:20?

Can you accept the truth that God has a good dream or plan in mind for you? (Jeremiah.29:11)

This next scripture is an indicator of what can sometimes happen once we make our own plans.

 ۞ Write out and meditate on Proverbs 16:9 (NASB)

Q. What can that verse mean to you personally?

 ۞ Look it up in a few different versions.
 ۞ Consider trying the writting techniques at the back of the book *on page 141.*
 ۞ Take time to pray for the requests that you have on your *Prayer Pages* in the back of this book.

Day Four – God Knows It All

Write out Psalm 139:4

Write out Psalm 147:5

Write out 1 John 3:20

Q. Do you see a theme in these verses as it relates to what God knows?

Q. Can you appreciate the gap between what you know and what God knows?

✡ Take time to thank God for knowing what is best for you.

✡ Take time to pray for the requests that you have on your *Prayer Pages* in the back of this book.

Day Five – Weekly Finale

Your goal this week was to understand what a *Worship Quest* is and also to study and personalize the word "worship."

✓ Take a moment to go back and reflect and refine your own definition of worship or on another definition that speaks to you.

We have studied the first half of the chorus from "More Than You Think I Am."

I'm more than you dream
More than you understand
Your days and your times
Were destined for our dance

Here are some key points to review and remember:

- God is more than we can dream or understand. He is beyond our comprehension. Yes, we should strive to know Him and to know His Word more. Yes, we should dream big and believe big. However, we must ultimately submit our thoughts and dreams to His will and ways. Remember, His ways and thoughts are higher than ours. (Isaiah 55:8-9)

- God "is able to do far more abundantly beyond all that we can ask or think, according to the power that works within us." (Ephesians 3:20)

- God is spirit, and those who worship Him must worship in spirit and in truth. (John 4:24)

- God is sovereign. That means that "He is the supreme ruler and authority, that He ordains whatever comes to pass, and that His divine purpose is always accomplished."[8] He is in charge. We can make our plans, but the Lord directs our steps. (Proverbs 16:9)

✧ God holds our days and our times in His hands because He is omniscient (all-knowing), and He sees the end from the beginning. (Psalm 139:4, 147:5, 1 John 3:20)

Add your own items to remember:

✧ _____

✧ _____

✧ _____

Review, meditate, write out Psalm 147:5

✧ Pray for the requests that you have on your *Prayer Pages* in the back of this book.

Session 2

Our Quest Continues

Worship is about what we love. What we live for. It's about who we are before God.

-Bob Kauflin, Worship Matters

Session Two: Our Quest Continues

 Prelude

Small Group – Connection Questions
(Try to be in groups no larger than 4 or 5. Allot 10 minutes.)

- Do you have a favorite worship song or hymn? Which song and why do you love it so much?
- Were you able to come up with your own definition of worship? If so, be bold and share. ☺

Video Listening Notes (12.5 minutes)

Worship

The overarching goal of this study is to grow closer to God as we expand our understanding of worship and explore His Word. The more we know God's Word, the better we can love and serve others.

Bob Kauflin, in his book *Worship Matters*, shares that "worship is about what we love. What we live for. It's about who we are before God." [1]

Worship is about what we love. Bob goes on to say that "while it's simplistic to say that worship is love, it's a fact that what we love most will determine what we genuinely worship." [2]

Yes, we can love other things and other people; "but we can't love anything in the right way unless we love God more." [3]

Four Questions to Consider (taken from Bob Kauflin's book, Worship Matters):

1. How do you know what you love most?

2. What do you spend most of your time doing?

3. Where does your mind drift to when you don't have anything to do?

4. What do you worship?

Your answers to those questions will lead you straight to the God or gods that you love and worship.[4]

In the first and greatest commandment (Matthew 22:37), we're commanded to love the Lord with all of our heart, soul and mind.

The reality is that we love better when we know God better because God is love. (1 John 4:8)

Worship is about our heart attitude. If you approach every day and every task with a heart to love and serve God, your life IS worship.

Shachah means to bow down or pay homage.

Proskuneo means to do reverence to and comes from the root words *pros* (to or toward) *and kuneo* (to kiss). [5]

We pay homage to God when we show special honor and respect toward Him.

Tear Bottles (Lachrymatory Bottles)

In Roman times, mourners would place tear bottles in burial tombs as symbols of respect.

During the Victorian period, in the 19th century, mourners had tear bottles with special stoppers that would let the tears evaporate. Once the tears were gone, the mourning period was over. There are some American Civil War stories of women saving their bottles of tears until their husbands returned from battle. The collected tears would represent how much they were loved and missed.

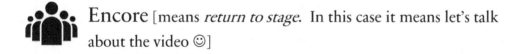

Encore [means *return to stage*. In this case it means let's talk about the video ☺]

Q. What stood out to you in the video teaching?

Q. Anything interesting or new?

Overture (Listen to the song. Full song lyrics are on page 15.)

Burn your name on my heart

Be still & trust my plan

I'm more than you think I am

I catch all your tears

Chorus Part 2

CHORUS
Part Two

He will be like a tree
planted by streams of water..
- Psalm 1:3a, NASB

This week's lesson will be focused on the second half of the chorus from "More Than You Think I Am." Here is the first lyric that we're studying:

♩♪ *I catch all your tears,*
burn your name on my heart

Read Psalm 56:8, the first documented reference about collecting tears in a bottle,.

The word "tears" is used 35 times in the Bible. Twenty-four times in the Old Testament and eleven in the New Testament.

"Today, lachrymatory bottles may also be called a tear bottle, tear catcher, tear vial, unguentaria, or unguentarium. There are also several less common spellings for lachrymatory, including lachrimatory...The tear bottle tradition has historically been a mourning tradition. Only in contemporary times have tears of joy and inspiration been captured." [6]

To study more about "tears," visit: https://www.gotquestions.org/tears-in-a-bottle.html

Q. As you consider what you have just learned about tear bottles, what are your thoughts on that scripture verse?

 Read Revelation 7:17 and Revelation 21:4a (the first sentence only)

Q. Which sentence is repeated?

Q. What do these scriptures teach us about tears? Other thoughts?

♫ *Be still and trust my plan*

The whole notion of *being still* runs counter to how we are built in general. Lord, we have so much to get done! Be still?

"Be still and trust" can seem like inactivity – like doing nothing – but it is quite the opposite. It actually takes *more* self-control to be still and trust God.

Read and write out Psalm 46:10.

If possible, have participants share that verse from a few different Bible versions.

Note that the NASB version says "cease striving." That means "stop stressing!" Charles Spurgeon says it can be translated "hold still."

In Exodus, chapter 14, Moses was leading the Israelites out of the desert and the Egyptians were chasing them. The Israelites were not happy with Moses and were telling him so. Here is Moses' reply.

Read Exodus 14:13-14. Write out Exodus 14:14.

Have participants share that verse from a few different Bible versions.

Instead of "keep silent," the New Living Translation says, "just stay calm." The King James Version says, "hold your peace."

Q. What do those scriptures tell us about being still and trusting? What is our part?

♩ *I'm more than you think I am*

That is the last line of the chorus. The lyric goes back to that idea that He is more than we can fully understand. He is beyond comprehension.

Q. Any initial thought on that lyric? Do you agree with it?

Here are a few quotes to consider about comprehending God and worship:

The late J. Vernon McGee once wrote that "attempting to define worship is a problem much the same as that of the soldier stationed on the West Coast, when his mother, a native of Kansas, wrote, saying, 'When you come home, please bring a souvenir that will tell me something of the Pacific Ocean which I have heard so much about.' So, when he went home he took her a bottle of sea water. Now that bottle of sea water may have said something about the ocean, but it told nothing of its vastness, of the breakers along the shore, nothing of the beauty of the sunlight on the whitecaps. It told nothing of the things of the deep, of the breeze that gently hovers. Neither can mere words adequately define the subject before us: worship." [7]

The incomprehensibility of God could lead to despair or apathy in the quest to know God, but the Bible also teaches that God is knowable. While God can never be exhaustively understood, he can be known truly, personally, and sufficiently. God is personal, has definite characteristics, and has personally revealed himself so that he can be truly known. The multiplication of grace and peace in our lives is dependent on knowing God (2 Pet. 1:2–3), and this knowledge provides sufficient resources for life and for becoming the people God wants us to be. – Erik Thoennes [8]

Application: Making the Lesson Practical

Discuss as a group or take home if time doesn't allow for discussion. If you are in multiple small groups, move to a full group discussion.

<u>What action steps can we list from the information that we have just studied?</u> Participants take a few minutes to look back over the lesson and find action steps that you can share with the group. Group leader, record ideas on a whiteboard if possible. Participants, write the shared responses here:

Here are a few examples:

- ✧ I need to take time this week to consider the four questions from the video.

- ✧ My part in faith is to be still and trust God. This is action not inaction.

⸮ Rest: Making the Lesson Personal

Be still and silently reflect on what you've learned today.

Q. Is there anything from the lesson today that you learned or should spend more time thinking or praying about?

See more reflection questions on page 24.

Prayer

Close out this session by praying for one another in large or small groups. Use your *Prayer Pages* in the back of this book to record and remember prayer requests.

Therefore, confess your sins to one another, and pray for one another so that you may be healed. The effective prayer of a righteous man can accomplish much.

– James 5:16, NASB

Personal Study: Going Deeper, Day by Day

Day One: Worship Review & Renew

Go back and review day one of last week's personal study. Specifically look at your personal definition of worship. If you haven't written out your own personal definition, take time to do so now. If you did write it out last week, rewrite it now and, if you like, add to it based on what you learned about worship in this week's group lesson.

☼ My personal definition of worship:

Meditate on Psalm 100 and choose a verse or word to write down and focus on throughout this coming week.

Why did you choose that verse or word?

OPTIONAL SOCIAL MEDIA ITEM (if applicable, ask group leader)

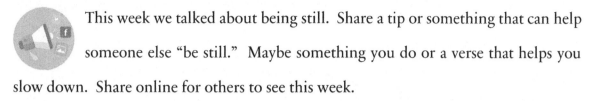 This week we talked about being still. Share a tip or something that can help someone else "be still." Maybe something you do or a verse that helps you slow down. Share online for others to see this week.

☼ Pray for the requests that you have on your *Prayer Pages* in the back of this book.

_____

Day Two: What or Who Do You Love?

Bob Kauflin's statement that "while it's simplistic to say that worship is love, it's a fact that what we love most will determine what we genuinely worship." [9]

Take time today, and throughout the week, to be introspective and write down your answers to these four questions (mentioned in your group lesson):

1. How do you know what you love most?

2. What do you spend most of your time doing?

3. Where does your mind drift to when you don't have anything to do?

4. What do you worship?

In answering those questions, what did you learn about yourself and what you love or worship most?

♢ Write Out Matthew 22:37

Q. Do your answers to the above questions reveal that you do love God with all of your heart, soul and mind? Where might you need to improve? For example, perhaps you place your marriage or your child first, above your relationship with Christ. You would want to make some adjustments to acknowledge God first.

♢ Pray for the requests that you have on your *Prayer Pages* in the back of this book.

Day Three: Words for Worship

The way that translators take the original Hebrew or Greek word and translate it into English words is noteworthy. When people are worshipping someone other than God, the English will be something like "bow down." When someone is worshipping God, they will use the word "worship."

Write out Genesis 23:7.

Write out Exodus 24:1.

One will read "worship" and the other says "bow down." Note that they are both from the same Hebrew word *shachah* yet they are worded or translated differently.

Write out Matthew 18:26.

Write out John 4:24.

The verse in Matthew reads "fell on his knees" while John reads as "worship." Note that they are both from the same Greek word *proskuneo*, yet they are worded/translated differently. Interesting, right?

In all cases in scripture, people are either worshipping God, other people or things. The same is true today. Watch out for idols which are things or people that you love more than God.

Q. How can you bow down or honor God in your relationships and activities? How can you reflect Christ with your heart attitude and worship?

✣ Pray for the requests that you have on your *Prayer Pages* in the back of this book.

Day Four: Be Still and Trust God's Plan

> "We need to find God,
>
> and he cannot be found in noise and restlessness.
>
> God is the friend of silence.
>
> See how nature - trees, flowers, grass - grows in silence;
>
> see the stars, the moon and the sun, how they move in silence."
>
> - Mother Teresa

God is a friend of silence...and we should endeavor to be that friend too. Challenge yourself today to be still and be silent. How long you can do that? Take a walk outside in nature. Be silent wherever you are, for as long as you can.

Write the number of minutes/hours that you were able to silent here: _____

If it helps you to read scripture while being still, here are key verses: Psalm 46:10, Exodus 14:14, Lamentations 3:24-26.

  ☿ Pray for the requests that you have on your *Prayer Pages* in the back of this book.

Day Five: Weekly Finale

This week we studied the second half of the chorus from our signature song, "More Than You Think I Am:"

I catch all your tears,
Burn your name on My 🎵
Be still and trust My pla
I'm more than you think I am.

Here are some key points to review and remember

- ⋄ What we love most will determine what we genuinely worship. [10]

- ⋄ Worship is about our heart attitude. If we approach every day and every task with a heart to love and serve God, our life IS worship. (Matthew 22:37)

- ⋄ Two new words for worship are *shachah*, which means to bow down or pay homage and *proskuneo*, which means to do reverence to. *Proskuneo* comes from the root words *pros* (to or toward) and *kuneo* (to kiss). [11]

- ⋄ God counts all our tears and sees our sorrow. (Psalm 56:8)

- ⋄ Being still and silent before God is not inactivity. (Exodus 14:14)

Review your notes from the group lesson and your last four days of personal time with God.

Q. What would you like to remember and take away from your studies this week?

ϙ   _____

ϙ   _____

Think about your personal definition of worship. If you haven't written one down, take time to do so. How can we worship God more and love Him more if we don't really know what worship means?

ϙ   Pray for the requests that you have on your *Prayer Pages* in the back of this book

BLANK SPACE! Have you tried any writing exercises? This is open space for you to try something new. Maybe take a picture and share it on the Worship Quest Facebook page or on your own local social media group that you may be doing this study with? #worshipquest

Session 3

Worship While You Work

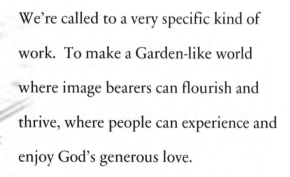

We're called to a very specific kind of work. To make a Garden-like world where image bearers can flourish and thrive, where people can experience and enjoy God's generous love.

-John Mark Comer, Garden City

Lesson Three: Worship While You Work

 Prelude

Small Group – Connection Questions

(Try to be in groups no larger than 4 or 5. Allot 10 minutes.)

- Share a little bit about yourself and what your current "work" status is. Do you stay at home or go out of the house to work? Are you retired?
- Do you think work is worship, worship is work, or neither?

Video Listening Notes (7 minutes)

Worship

Review: *Shachah* means to bow down or pay homage.

Proskuneo means to do reverence to and comes from the root words pros (to or toward) and kuneo (to kiss). [1]

New: *abad* occurs 7X in the Old Testament (Hebrew) and it means "to work, serve" or "to make, do." [2]

The real question is "what is my attitude like" when I'm working?

And so it is with you... we are in charge of our attitude. This is the last line of the poem titled "Attitude" by Charles Swindoll

Five More Questions to Consider (taken from Bob Kauflin's book, Worship Matters):

1. What are you passionate about?

2. What do you spend your money on?

3. What makes you angry when you don't get it?

4. What do you feel depressed without?

5. What do you fear losing the most?

 Encore [means *return to stage*. In this case it means let's talk about the video ☺]

Q. What stood out to you in the video teaching?

Overture (Listen to the song. Full song lyrics are on page 15)

Lyrics & Lessons (Verse One)

You'd be amazed the places that I go

to be with you where you are.

So forget what you've heard

what you think that you know

there's a lot about me that's never been told.

You always think I'm somewhere

on a mountaintop but never think behind bars

Verse 1

VERSE ONE

He will be like a tree
planted by streams of water..
- Psalm 1:3a, NASB

Today we investigate verse one of "More Than You Think I Am."

You always think I'm somewhei
on a mountaintop
But never think, behind bars

Q. What do you think this lyric could mean? Discuss.

Behind Bars

I can't speak for the authors of this song or know for certain what they meant by this lyric. What I can tell you is that this line alone could be studied for weeks! How many times were the disciples behind bars, Paul in particular? What did they learn behind bars? Was God there for them? Absolutely.

 In Genesis chapter 39, Joseph is sent to prison after Potiphar's wife lies and tells her husband that he tried to seduce her.

Read Genesis 39:19-23. Take special notice of verse 21 and 23b starting with "because."

This verse is the first mention of prison or jail in the Bible. In this instance, we see God extending kindness, giving Joseph favor and allowing him to prosper. God meets people behind prison bars.

 Read 1 Kings 20:26-29. Write out 1 Kings 20:28b again, starting with the word "because" and up until the word "valleys."

In that situation, the Arameans (Syrians) had said that God was the god of the mountains, not the valleys. And for this reason, God gave the Israelites victory over them and they were defeated. In those days (not unlike today), it was common for people to make up their own gods. Charles Spurgeon noted that "while the Syrians thus ascribed their defeat unto Jehovah, *they made a great mistake as to His character*, for they supposed Him to be a local God, like their own imaginary deities. They had gods for the mountains and gods for the lesser hills, gods for the rivers, gods for the fields, gods for their houses, gods for their gardens and these so-called gods were powerless out of their own sphere. They imagined the only living and true God to be a god like their idols." [3] (Italics mine)

Q. How can this verse serve as a word of caution or warning for us?

Just like the Arameans, it would be a mistake for us to think that God is a "local" god. That's He only has power and reigns in certain places. He is the God of both the mountains and the valleys. He meets people in high and low places, in good and bad circumstances. That means He is on the mountain tops and behind bars, whether those be actual jail bars or bars of our own making (Romans 7:14-25).

 *You'd be amazed the places that I go,*
to be with you, where you are.

Q. What does this lyric say to you?

Read Matthew 9:10-13.

Q. What was Jesus' response to their question in verse 11?

In that passage, the Pharisees (religious people) were disgusted that Jesus was hanging out with the tax collectors and the sinners of the day. Let's just say that the Pharisees were amazed that Jesus chose to keep company with such a motley crew. If you study Jesus long enough, you'll find out that such was the case more often than not.

In contrast, the Pharisees were very judgmental toward others and very concerned about keeping up appearances. They had a clear idea of what holy people should and should not do. They didn't think Jesus should be spending time with "those" people. How about you?

Q. In your current situation, do you have any contact with people who don't look like you or agree with you?

Q. Where do you need to show more grace toward people that look, feel and act differently than I do?

Q. Do you love people where they are at or would you love them more when they get to where you think they should be?

Jesus spent time with the outcast, the sinners – and so should we.

   Read Psalm 139:7-10.

Q. How does it make you feel, knowing that God is everywhere, that you can't hide from Him?

Q. Why might some people find His constant presence a bit scary?

So forget what you've heard
What you think that you know
There's a lot about Me
That's never been told

It would be pure speculation to tell you what this lyric means but my sense is that we need to be teachable and willing to be corrected when our thinking (theology) doesn't line up with the truth of the Word of God. We can "think" something and be completely wrong in our thinking. God wants His thoughts to be our thoughts and that is going to depend on us knowing Him through His Word, more and more.

Let's just agree that we don't know everything and that we never will.

Q. Any other thoughts on these lyrics?

 Application: Making the Lesson Practical

Discuss as a group or take home if time doesn't allow for that. If you are in multiple small groups, move to a full group discussion.

What action steps can we list from the information that we have just studied? Participants take a few minutes to look back over the lesson and find action steps that you can share with the group. Group leader, record ideas on a whiteboard if possible. Participants, write the shared responses here:

Rest: Making the Lesson Personal (5 minutes)

Silently review what has been shared and discussed today.

Q. Is there anything from the lesson today that you learned or should spend more time thinking or praying about?

Q. Is there a verse or a question that stood out to you? If so, note that now.

Prayer

Close out this session by praying for one another in large or small groups. Use your *Prayer Pages* in the back of this book to record and remember the prayer requests.

With all prayer and petition pray at all times in the Spirit, and with this in view, be on the alert with all perseverance and petition for all the saints. – Ephesians 6:18, NASB

Day One: Your work is worship?

Our Hebrew word for worship this week is _____ which means "to work, serve" or "to make, do." [4]

The Bible opens up with God working and creating (Genesis 1:1-15).

    ✡   Read/write out Genesis 1:31.

Q. What did God think about His work?

In Genesis we see that God put Adam and Eve in the garden to cultivate it and keep it (Gen. 2:15). God entrusted people with the garden...and the work. You might remember that didn't go so well because they didn't follow God's direction. Anyhow, God was the first worker and He calls us to work with Him and for Him.

Q. What is your attitude about work like? Write out Colossians 3:23.

Q. As it relates to the idea of working, what can you take away from that verse?

Q. Do you need to make any adjustments to the way you work or the attitude that you bring into your work?

☼ Write out John 4:34:

Just like Jesus, our goal should be to "accomplish His work."

☼ Pray for the requests that you have on your *Prayer Pages* in the back of this book.

Day Two: What do you worship?

Last week you were given four questions to help you get to the bottom of what or who it is that you worship. Take time today, and throughout this week, to be introspective and write down your answers to these five additional questions (mentioned in your group video lesson).

1. What are you passionate about?

2. What do you spend your money on?

3. What makes you angry when you don't get it?

4. What do you feel depressed without?

5. What do you fear losing the most?

Spend some time processing your answers to those five questions and the four questions from last week.

✡ Do you see trends or themes in the things that you worship, other than God?

✡ How can you rearrange your priorities and time so you are giving God first place in your life?

✡ Write Out Matthew 22:37

✡ Do your answers to the above questions reveal that you do love God with all of your heart, soul and mind? Where might you need to improve?

This week we talked about having a good attitude while we work. Share a tip or practical way that we can communicate a good attitude to others, while we are working (serving). Share online for others to see this week.

☼ Pray for the requests that you have on your *Prayer Pages* in the back of this book.

☼ Have you tried any creative writing techniques from the back of the book? Maybe today is the day. ☺

Day Three: Attitude Adjustment?

We've studied the origin of work in scriptures and touched on the importance of our working with the right attitude. Maybe you already have a great attitude about serving and working. If so, skip ahead! Chances are that we can all use a tune-up. I know I do.

✧ Read/write out Philippians 2:3-5

✧ Read/write out Philippians 2:14

Q. What can we learn from those verses, as it relates to proper attitude? How does a proper attitude impact our work?

Q. As a rule, do you value (place) others above yourself?

Q. Do you do everything without grumbling or complaining?

Q. If you had to rank your attitude from 1 to 10 (1 being very cranky and 10 being Miss Mary Sunshine), what number would you give yourself?

Q. Recognizing that others are watching you and some will replicate your behavior, are you setting a good example as a worker and follower of Christ?

Take some time now to review your answers as it relates to the verses above.

Q. What adjustments do you think you need to make to have a more Christlike attitude?

✧ Pray for the requests that you have on your *Prayer Pages* in the back of this book.

Day Four: Friend of Sinners?

Take time today to go back and review the notes and verses from your group lesson (Genesis 39:19, 1 Kings 20:28 and Matthew 9:10-13).

Review your answers, or record your answers now that you have time, to the questions regarding sinners and grace on page 70 and 71.

♩ **Song Search** (Google, YouTube, Siri, Alexa, whatever floats your boat): "Jesus, Friend of Sinners" by Casting Crowns

☼ Pray for the requests that you have on your *Prayer Pages* in the back of this book.

Day Five: Weekly Finale

Some of the learning objectives that we have covered this week were to:

- ♥ Learn another word for worship, *abad*, which means to work, serve, make or do.

- ♥ Connect your "work" with your "worship."

- ♥ Ask more questions (5) and continue to look at who or what you really worship.

- ♥ Check your attitudes, particularly as they relate to your work.

- ♥ Remember that God is not a "local" god. He is everywhere. In the hills and valleys; in prisons and hard places.

- ♥ Remember that Jesus was criticized for keeping company with the sinners.

- ♥ Think about being intentional about who you spend time with.

Q. How did you do on the items above?

Take time today to review your work from this week: the group lesson and your daily studies. Finish up anything that may be left undone. Spend time on areas that you would like to focus on more.

- ♥ Pray for the requests that you have on your *Prayer Pages* in the back of this book.

Session  4

Forgiveness & Friendship

This is My commandment, that you love one another, just as I have loved you. Greater love has no one than this, that one lay down his life for his friends.

-John. 15:12-13, NASB

Lesson Four: Forgiveness & Friendship

 Prelude

Small Group – Connection Questions
(Try to be in groups no larger than 4 or 5. Allot 10 minutes.)

- Do you or have you ever thought of God as a harsh judge?

- Do you consider God to be your friend? If yes, explain what that looks like in your life.

Video Listening Notes (8.5 minutes)

Lesson ONE Highlights:

- Worship is central to our life purpose.

- Worship is a verb, an intention of the heart, an action.

- Worship is a lifestyle that should extend into every waking moment of our life.

- "Worship is defined by the priority we place on who God is in our lives and where God is in our list of priorities." - Delesslyn Kennebrew

- "Every deed, every action that we perform can be done to the glory of God and can serve as worship." - Vines Dictionary's

- "Worship is about what we love. What we live for. It's about who we are before God." – Bob Kauflin
- Worship is about our heart attitude. If you approach every day and every task with a heart to love and serve God, your life IS worship.

Lesson TWO Highlights:

- The Hebrew word for worship, *shachah*, means to bow down or pay homage or respect.
- The Greek word for worship, *proskuneo*, means to do reverence to and comes from the root words *pros* and *kuneo* which mean "to move toward" and "to kiss."

Lesson THREE Highlights:

- The Hebrew word for worship, *abad*, means to work, serve or to make, do.
- It's important to connect our work with our worship.
- We need to check our attitudes, particularly as they relate to our work.

This Week:

- Another Greek word for worship is *sebasma* which comes from the Greek root word *sebazomal* meaning "to fear" or "to have reverential awe."
- See God as who He really is, a loving, forgiving Father and a friend who longs to be in a relationship with you.

Encore

[means *return to stage*. In this case it means let's talk about the video ☺]

Q. Any thoughts on the video that you just watched? As we look back over the last few weeks of our study, what do you think has been the most interesting or helpful?

 Overture (Listen to the song. Full song lyrics are on page 15)

Lyrics & Lessons (Verse Two)

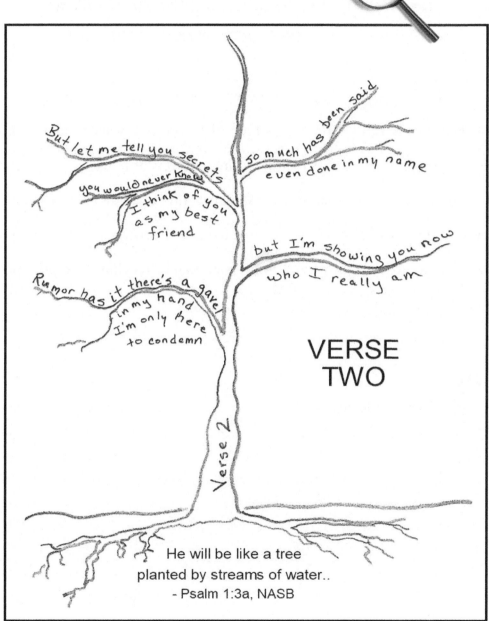

Today we investigate verse two of our signature song.

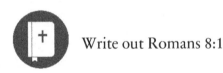 *Rumor has it there's a gavel in My hand*
I'm only here to condemn.

It is true that God is our Judge and we will all have to give an account of ourselves to Him (Ecclesiastes 12:14, Romans 14:12). That can be a scary thought, however, the important thing to focus on is that, if we are followers of Jesus, we are forgiven and no longer condemned. Jesus died as a sinless man, to give us access to His Father and heaven forever. If this is a new idea to you or if you don't understand the concept, please reach out to your group leader or a trusted Christian friend after class, for on this principal lies our entire faith.

Write out Romans 8:1

You are "in Christ" if you admit that you have sinned (we all have, Romans 3:23); if you believe that Jesus died for you, to forgive you of those sins; and if you have told someone (confessed) that Jesus is now Lord of your life.

Romans 8:1 says that if you are "in Christ" you are no longer under condemnation. That means you are no longer guilty. You have been declared righteous or innocent of all charges! When we sin, we still confess them and ask for forgiveness. What we don't do is continue to beat ourselves up or others, for that matter, for sins we have confessed. We move on. We forgive ourselves and others so we can live freely and love lavishly.

♫ *But let Me tell you secrets*
you would never know
I think of you as My best friend

Let's take time and look at how the word "friend" is used in scripture. If you search the word "friend" in Biblegateway.com, in the New American Standard Bible (NASB) version, it records that "friend" is used 120 times in scripture. Eighty-seven times in the Old Testament and thirty-three in the New Testament.

Q. *What are some qualities of a good friend?* Leader, record the participants answers to this question. Participants take notes here.

The scriptures listed below are the main verses regarding Jesus and friendship, from the Old Testament through the New Testament, in the order in which they appear. In your group, take turns reading aloud the items listed below:

- ☿ Moses characterized his own relationship with God as being "face to face, just as a man speaks to a friend." Moses wrote the book of Exodus (Exodus 33:11).

- ☿ Isaiah referred to Abraham as God's friend (Isaiah 41:8).

- ☿ The author of 2 Chronicles noted that the land of Israel was given to Abraham, God's friend forever (2 Chronicles 20:7).

- ⚘ Jesus remarked about how He was being referred to by others as "a friend of tax collectors and sinners" (Matthew 11:19 and Luke 7:34).

- ⚘ When Jesus healed the paralytic, who had been lowered down from a roof into the house where Jesus was at, he called him friend (Luke 5:20).

- ⚘ Jesus called His disciples friends (Luke 12:4).

- ⚘ John recalls Jesus referring to Lazarus as a friend (John 11:11).

- ⚘ Abraham (formerly called Abram) was referred to as a "friend of God" by James, Jesus' brother (James 2:23).

Moses, Abraham, Lazarus, the paralytic, and the disciples. Those are the only people specifically referred to as a "friend" in scripture. And he never specifically addressed anyone as His "best" friend.

Jesus' definitive word on the subject can be found in a key passage of scripture, John 15:12-17. In the New American Standard Bible (NASB), this section of scripture is titled as the "Disciples' Relation to Each Other."

Read John 15:12-17. Participants take turns reading the verses.

v. 12 "This is My commandment, that you love one another, just as I have loved you.

v. 13 Greater love has no one than this, that one lay down his life for his *friends.*

v. 14 You are *My friends if* you do what I command you.

v. 15 No longer do I call you slaves, for the slave does not know what his master is doing; but *I have called you friends,* or all things that I have heard from My Father I have made known to you.

v. 16 You did not choose Me but I chose you, and appointed you that you would go and bear fruit, and that your fruit would remain, so that whatever you ask of the Father in My name He may give to you.

v. 17 This I command you, that you love one another." (John 15:12-17, NASB, emphasis added, mine)

Q. The John 15 passage is bookended with one phrase comprised of 5 words. Look in verses twelve and seventeen. What is the key phrase? _____ _____ _____ _____ _____.

Q. In the center, verse 14, a conditional statement is made. We are God's friends if we do what? _____

Q. This is such a great passage. Look it over again. What lessons or actions can we take away from it?

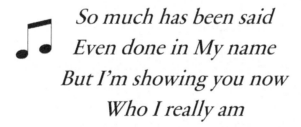

So much has been said
Even done in My name
But I'm showing you now
Who I really am

As was mentioned in the opening video, people say things and do things in the name of God. Sometimes that is a good thing and sometimes it is not.

Q. How can you really know who God is?

Now that's a great question. I hope you all were able to conclude that you can only really know who God is by studying the Word of God. In fact, everything that you think about God needs to be confirmed in scripture. Don't take anyone else's word because we are human and not without fault.

 Application: Making the Lesson Practical

Discuss as a group or take home, if time doesn't allow for group discussion. If you are normally in multiple small groups, move to a *full group discussion.*

What action steps can we list from the information that we have just studied? Participants take a few minutes to look back over the lesson and find action steps that you can share with the group. Group leader, record ideas on a whiteboard if possible. Participants, write the shared responses here:

Rest: Making the Lesson Personal (3-5 minutes)

Silently review what has been shared and discussed today.

Q. Is there anything from the lesson today that you learned or should spend more time thinking or praying about?

Q. Is there a verse or a question that stood out to you? If so, note that now.

Prayer

Close out this session by praying for one another in large or small groups. Use your Prayer Pages in the back of this book to record and remember the prayer requests.

For this reason I too, having heard of the faith in the Lord Jesus which exists among you and your love for all the saints, do not cease giving thanks for you, while making mention of you in my prayers; - Ephesians 1:15-16, NASB

Day One: Another Word for Worship

In this week's video, we reviewed the Hebrew and Greek words that we have learned for the word "worship." Again, it really is an eye-opening exercise to study the original meaning of words in the Bible. If you look up the word "worship" in a Bible concordance, there are eleven different Hebrew and Greek words for worship. So far, we've studied *shachah, proskuneo* and *abad*.

Your new word for worship this week is *sebasma* which comes from the Greek root word *sebazomal* meaning "to fear" or "to have reverential awe."

> To fear God is not to shrink back from Him in terror. To fear God is to have a deep reverence for Him, and to stand in awe at His holiness and majesty and power and love. Only then will we love and serve and worship Him as we should. - Billy Graham [1]

A healthy fear, reverence and awe of God is directly linked to our love and worship of God. We can't love and worship God as we should if we don't have a healthy fear and reverence for Him. "A true fear of the Lord realizes you can't run from God, and the only option is to run to him. When you do, you find the embracing arms of a loving Father." [2]

    ☼ Reflect on this new word, *sebasma*, and its definition for a few minutes.

Q. Are you afraid of God or do you fear Him?

Q. What do you think it means, in practice, "to fear" God or to "have reverential awe?"

Q. Do you think you have a healthy or unhealthy fear of the Lord? Do you know the difference between the two, if so, what is it?

Write out and meditate on Proverbs 9:10.

☼ Pray over what you have just studied and learned. Ask God to help you retain what you need to for real transformation in your life. Pray also for the requests that you have on your *Prayer Pages* in the back of this book.

OPTIONAL SOCIAL MEDIA ITEM (if applicable, ask group leader)

 This week, in our group lesson, we talked about friendship. What qualities, in your closest friends, do you most appreciate? Share online for others to see this week.

Day Two: Here Comes the Judge

Therefore, there is now no condemnation for those who are in Christ Jesus.

- Romans 8:1, NASB

In your group study this week, we looked at the song lyric: "rumor has it there's a gavel in my hand. I'm only here to condemn." There's some truth to that lyric. Many people do feel that God is a heavy-handed, buzz killer and that being a Christian is all about having to follow rules and living a life of no joy.

They likely feel that way because they have encountered Christians who are very judgmental and who will be the first ones to squash their behavior by tossing a scripture verse their way. Those Christians don't exude joy and they are the first to call out the rule breakers and show others how holy they are. The Pharisees did that to Jesus too and it didn't go over well. In any case, it's easy to see why people view God as the mean dad just waiting to clobber them.

Perhaps you struggle with feeling condemned, in general, or you struggle with feeling condemned, specifically, and repeatedly beat yourself up over things that you have done in the past. You did something horrible. You confessed the sin to God and asked for forgiveness but everyone once in a while you dredge it back up and tell yourself what a horrible person you are for what you did and how you're not worthy of anything good because you did something so bad. Moreover, why should anyone love you because you are such a bad person? Does that ring a bell? If you do not struggle with condemnation, someone that you know does. Living life with a constant feeling that you are condemned or by revisiting every sin you've committed is not biblical and is certainly not healthy.

As discussed in this week's lesson, Jesus paid the price by dying on the cross for your sins and mind. The debt was paid in full. Yes, God is our Judge and He sees our sin. We are accountable for them. However, once we confess our sins, they are forgiven. Done with. Reconciled. It says so in the Bible. When you keep on punishing yourself, that it is a form of unbelief. Also called sin. When God says he forgives us and our sins have been removed from us "as far at the East is from the West (Psalm 103:12)," we need to believe

Him and adjust our thinking accordingly. Each time you punish yourself for things you've done in the past, you are essentially telling God that you don't believe that He forgave you. Yikes!

If we confess our sins, He is faithful and righteous to forgive us our sins and to cleanse us from all unrighteousness. -1 John 1:9

Write that scripture out here:

Take some time today to see if you need to adjust your thinking and stop beating yourself up for sins you've confessed to God yet you're still hanging on to. If you are not caught in this trap, maybe you can remind someone else who struggles with this habit.

- ✧ Pray over what you have just studied and learned. Are you a judgmental Christian that reminds others of their past mistakes? How is your friendship with God these days? Ask God to help you retain what you need to for real transformation in your life. Pray also for the requests that you have on your *Prayer Pages* in the back of this book.

Day Three: The Big "If"

You are *My friends if* you do what I command you. -John 15:14, NASB (emphasis added, mine)

This is the conditional verse that was discussed in your group study this week. It basically means that I am God's friend IF I do what He commands. I'm calling this the "Big If," because the "if" depends on me doing what God commands. In other words, it boils down to me being obedient. Obedient. That's not a popular word. I know. Nonetheless, it is vitally important.

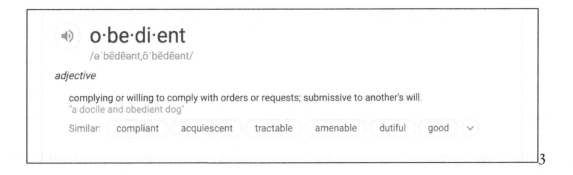

When someone thinks of commands, in the biblical sense, they often think back to Moses' Ten Commandments. In the first five books of the Bible, the Torah or Pentateuch, there were 613 commands. In the New Testament there are approximately

1,050.[4] Holy cats. That is a lot of commands for us to follow. What does that mean for us today?

Consider these two New Testament passages:

A new commandment I give to you, that you love one another, even as I have loved you, that you also love one another. By this all men will know that you are My disciples, if you have love for one another. – John 13:34-35, NASB

One of them, a lawyer, asked Him a question, testing Him, "Teacher, which is the great commandment in the Law?" And He said to him, "'You shall love the Lord your God with all your heart, and with all your soul, and with all your mind.' This is the great and foremost commandment. The second is like it, 'You shall love your neighbor as yourself.' On these two commandments depend the whole Law and the Prophets." – Matthew 22:35-40, NASB

You can see that "love" is at the center of these verses and that Jesus pointed out that the great commandment is for us to love God with all of our heart, soul and our mind and the second has to do with us loving our neighbors.

Reflect on these verses today and inventory yourself as it relates to loving God and others. Slow yourself down and be introspective.

Q. Would you say you are submissive to God's will (obedient) in your life or do you tend to do things your way?

Q. Do you love God with all of your heart, soul and mind? Where might you need to improve on that?

Q. Would those close to you describe you as loving? Are your actions and words loving?

Q. How loving are you toward your neighbors? How often do you serve your neighbors (others) in specific ways?

Q. Are you obedient to God meaning that you submit to God's will or are you in charge of your life and you do it your way?

Try to keep John 13:34-35 in view (print it, screenshot it, post it someplace you will see it) as you go about your week and think about your personal inventory questions.

☼ Pray over what you have just studied and learned. Ask God to help you retain what you need to for real transformation in your life. Pray also for the requests that you have on your *Prayer Pages* in the back of this book.

Day Four: I AM

I think one of the foremost lessons from the second chorus is that we need to know the truth of who God is, not based on what others say or do, but based on what the Bible says. He wants us to know who He really is and any time we try to figure out who He is based on someone else's filter or experience, we run into the danger of being misinformed.

That last line of verse two: "I'm showing you now, who I really am."

I am. Two very important words in the Bible. That two-word combination appears over 300 times in the Bible. They serve as bookends by appearing in the first book, Genesis 15:1, and then also in the last book, in Revelation 22:16. You could do an exhaustive study on this topic but for today's purposes, we're just going to look at some of the key I AM statements.

First, let's look at the bookends, the first and last I AM statements:

- ☿ Genesis 15:1, "After these things the word of the Lord came to Abram in a vision, saying, "Do not fear, Abram, I am a shield to you; Your reward shall be very great."

- ☿ Revelation 22:16, "I, Jesus, have sent My angel to testify to you these things for the churches. I am the root and the descendant of David, the bright morning star."

That last I AM statement ties all of the Bible together. Matthew opens his gospel by calling Jesus, "the son of David, the son of Abraham" (Matthew 1:1). Jesus' arrival was prophesied hundreds of years before He came. He descended from the line of Abraham and David. The more you study the Bible the more you will discover the fascinating linkage between the Old and New Testaments.

Here are just a few I AM statements to reflect on today, from the book of John.
- ☿ "I am the bread of life." (John 6:35, 41, 48, 51)
- ☿ "I am the light of the world." (John 8:12)
- ☿ "I am the door of the sheep." (John 10:7,9)
- ☿ "I am the resurrection and the life." (John 11:25)
- ☿ "I am the good shepherd." (John 10:11,14)
- ☿ "I am the way, the truth, and the life." (John 14:6)
- ☿ "I am the true vine." (John 15:1,5)

Look up these verses and try to find one that stands out to you. Maybe there is a verse that you find comforting. Maybe there is a verse that you've never read before or one that meets a specific need that you have today.

Write it out here:

⋄ Pray over what you have just studied and learned. Ask God to help you retain what you need to for real transformation in your life. Pray also for the requests that you have on your *Prayer Pages* in the back of this book.

Day Five: Weekly Finale

Some of the learning objectives that we have covered this week were:

- If you are in Christ (you follow Christ), your sins are forgiven, and you are no longer condemned. (Romans 8:1)

- Once you have confessed your sins, don't keep beating yourself up.

- The quality of your friendship with God is directly related to your obedience to His commands. (John 15)

- God calls you to love one another. (John 13:34-35, John 15)

- God chose you and appoints you to go bear fruit. (John 15)

- The new word for worship this week, *sebasma,* means to fear or to have reverential awe.

- The fear of the Lord is the beginning of wisdom. (Proverbs 9:10)

- Jesus said the great commandment is to love God will all of your heart, soul and mind and to love your neighbor as yourself. (Matthew 22:35-40)

- There are over 300 "I AM" statements in the Bible and you can know the truth of who God really is by studying the Bible.

Q. How did you do on the items above?

Take time today to review all of your work from this week: the group lesson, your daily studies. Finish up anything that may be left undone. Spend time on areas that you would like to focus on more.

♢ Pray for the requests that you have on your *Prayer Pages* in the back of this book.

Session 5

20/20 Vision

THE SPIRIT OF THE LORD IS UPON ME,

BECAUSE HE ANOINTED ME TO BRING GOOD NEWS TO THE POOR.

HE HAS SENT ME TO PROCLAIM RELEASE TO CAPTIVES,

AND RECOVERY OF SIGHT TO THE BLIND,

TO SET FREE THOSE WHO ARE OPPRESSED,

TO PROCLAIM THE FAVORABLE YEAR OF THE LORD."

-Luke 4:18-19, NASB

Session Five: 20/20 Vision

 Prelude

Small Group – Connection Questions
(Try to be in groups no larger than 4 or 5. Allot 10 minutes.)

- Make sure that you all know one another.

- Do you wear eyeglasses? If yes, how old were you when you started wearing them and why did you need them?

- How good are you at finding 3D images hidden in stereograms (the posters that look like tiled patterns but have images hidden in them)?

Video Listening Notes (10 minutes)

God wants an "all access" pass into your life and, actually, He has one.

God wants us to recognize that we don't have His 20/20 vision.

Jehovah Raah means the Lord that heals.

You would see a name and then a function or an attribute which was tied to the name.

El Roi, which is commonly translated as "the God who sees" or "the God who sees me."

El Roi occurs only once in scripture, in Genesis 16:13.

Ishmael means "God hears."

And then Hagar "called the name of the Lord who spoke to her, 'you are a God who sees.'" -Genesis 16:13a, NASB

When we hide in Him, versus hide from Him, He will give us a better, clearer vision of others and, most especially of Himself and of His love for us.

"Even if our gospel is veiled, it is veiled to those who are perishing, in whose case the god of this world has blinded the eyes of the unbelieving so that they might not see the light of the gospel of the glory of Christ, who is the image of God." -2 Cor 4:3-4, NASB

Encore

[means *return to stage*. In this case it means let's talk about the video ☺]

Q. Any thoughts on the video you just watched?

Overture (Listen to the song. Full song lyrics are on page 15)

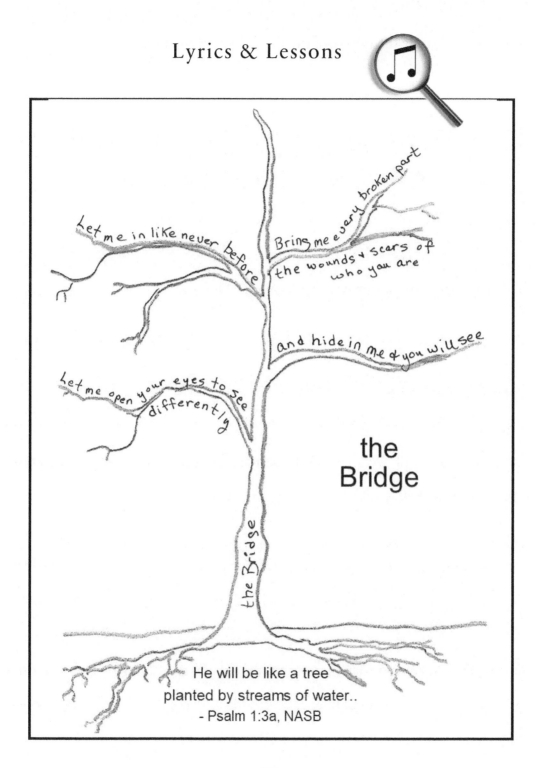

Let me in like never before

Bring me every broken part

the wounds & scars of who you are

and hide in me & you will see

Let me open your eyes to see differently

the Bridge

the Bridge

the
Bridge

He will be like a tree
planted by streams of water..
- Psalm 1:3a, NASB

Today we will study the bridge of the song. Here is the first line:

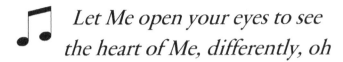

Let Me open your eyes to see
the heart of Me, differently, oh

Q. What do you think this lyric could mean? Discuss.

Open Your Eyes to See

The first mention of "eyes" in the Bible is in Genesis. Read Genesis 3. Look up the following verses below (NASB) and fill in the blanks.

For God knows that in the day you eat from it your _____ will be opened, and you will be like _____, knowing good and evil." - Genesis 3:5, NASB

When the woman saw that the tree was good for food, and that it was a delight to the _____, and that the tree was desirable to make *one* _____, she took from its fruit and ate; and she gave also to her husband with her, and he ate. - Genesis 3:6, NASB

Then the _____ of both of them were opened, and they knew that they were

_____; and they sewed fig leaves together and made themselves loin coverings. - Genesis 3:7, NASB

Q. Why did Eve take a bite of the apple?

Q. What observations can we make from these passages?

Vision Problems

The Bible mentions people having eyes but not being able to see. Read the following verses:

They have mouths, but they cannot speak;

They have eyes, but they cannot see; - Psalm 115:5

They have mouths, but they do not speak;

They have eyes, but they do not see; - Psalm 135:16

Then the eyes of the blind will be opened

And the ears of the deaf will be unstopped. – Isaiah 35:5

Q. What do you think is meant by these verses?

Write out Proverbs 21:2

Q. What does that verse say to you?

♫ *Let Me in like never before.*
Bring Me every broken part
the wounds and scars of who you are...

Let Me In

This idea, of letting Him in, goes back to last week's lesson and personal study day #3.

Obedience = submission to another's will.

Letting Him in means to surrender, obey, submit. Unpopular yet necessary words in the spiritual life. Have you surrendered your life to God or are you still in charge of your life and wanting to do things your way?

At the root of wanting to do things your way is control and fear. You can trust God and let go. You can trust God and let Him into your most secret places.

Read and write out Jeremiah 17:7-8. Does verse 7 ring any bells for you (remind you of anything?)

What specific benefits of trusting in the Lord do we find in these verses?

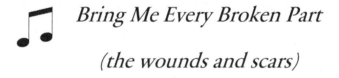 *Bring Me Every Broken Part*

(the wounds and scars)

Q. Has He healed a wound or scar that you have, that you are willing to share with the group?

Read Psalm 147:3

Q. If you consider that verse, does it make sense to bring Him all your broken parts? How do you think he heals and binds up wounds, just based on what you've experienced personally?

 And hide in Me and you will see

What does hiding in Christ look like? When we realize that God is our hiding place, our refuge, our safety and, at the same time, we realize that in that hiding place all of us is laid bare; we converge on a new level of intimacy with God.

Read Hebrews 4:13

Read Psalm 32:7

Q. Do you have any other thoughts about hiding in Christ?

Application: Making the Lesson Practical

Discuss as a group or take home if time doesn't allow for that. If you are in multiple small groups, move to a full group discussion.

What action steps can we list from the information that we have just studied? Participants take a few minutes to look back over the lesson and find action steps that you can share with the group. Group leader, record ideas on a whiteboard if possible. Participants, write the shared responses here:

⸂ Rest: Making the Lesson Personal (5 minutes)

Silently review what has been shared and discussed today.

Q. Is there anything from the lesson today that you learned or should spend more time thinking or praying about?

Q. Is there a verse or a question that stood out to you? If so, note that now.

Prayer

Close out this session by praying for one another in large or small groups. Use your Prayer Pages in the back of this book to record and remember the prayer requests.

Then you will call upon Me and come and pray to Me, and I will listen to you.

– Jeremiah 29:12, NASB

Personal Study: Going Deeper, Day by Day

Day One: Let God In

If someone shows up to your house and knocks on your front door, you either let the person in or you don't. You either acknowledge that someone is knocking on the door, or you pretend like no one is there. Those are really your only two options.

The same is true with Jesus. He is knocking (Rev. 3:20) and you can either let Him into your life or you can pretend like He isn't there. Again, He wants an All Access Pass into your life, but you have the same two choices that I just mentioned. The choice comes down to you. It's called free will.

Let's say that you let Him in. You're in Bible study for heaven's sake so you have either let Him in already or you're at least considering it!

How far do you bring Him into your house? Just into the foyer? Or maybe into the living room? Or do you share a meal with Him at your kitchen table. Is there surface conversation or do you pour out all your concerns and questions? How long is He invited to stay?

Think about that scenario today.

I'm going to circle back to the group lesson from our first week together. Let's go back to Ephesians 3:14-21. Read that passage and then write out verse 17.

That passage was the apostle Paul's prayer for every believer, that we would let Christ dwell richly in our hearts and that we would grow in our understanding of how deep and wide, and high and long the love of Christ is for us and specifically for you. This is what happens when you let Him into your life and your heart.

As you meditate on that today, you're love quotient will grow and so will your desire to worship God more and more and more.

- ☼ Pray over what you have just studied and learned. Ask God to help you retain what you need to for real transformation in your life. Pray also for the requests that you have on your *Prayer Pages* in the back of this book.

Since this is the last week with a formal lesson, consider these last several weeks of the study. Share your favorite highlight and think about who you can thank for making it special.

Day Two: Open Your Eyes

Today's lesson might be a bit of a sticky wicket but I'm going to go there anyhow. Although most people that do a Bible study are Jesus followers, not everyone is, therefore I should assume that some of you "have eyes but do not see" as mentioned in Psalm 135:16 and Psalm 135:16. Some of you are considering Christ and the claims for Christ but you haven't surrendered your life or your heart to Him. That's okay and I'm so glad you're doing this study.

If you are not a believer in Jesus yet, this idea might actually seem crazy or be offensive to you. I don't want to stir up trouble, but is it possible that there are things around you that you don't see quite as others see them?

In this week's video, I mentioned 2 Corinthians 4:4 and how that passage states that the enemy, Satan, has blinded some from believing in the gospel of Jesus Christ. That is why some people cannot understand or "see" what is happening around them, from a spiritual perspective, with their spiritual eyesight.

Read 2 Corinthians 4:4 (NASB) and fill in the blanks:

"even if our gospel is veiled, it is veiled to those who are perishing, in whose case the god of this world has blinded _____ _____of the unbelieving so that they might not see the light of the gospel of the glory of Christ, who is the image of God."

If you were to do a word study on "mind" (remember there are instructions on how to do a word study on the Worship Quest website), you would discover that the Greek word for mind is "noema" which means thought or purpose.[1] If you circle back to the scripture and substitute those words where the word "mind" is, the scripture now reads that the "god of this world has blinded my thoughts or purpose." Think about that for a bit.

The Vine's Dictionary gives us an even broader understanding of what it means when we're talking about the enemy blinding minds. Vines states that *nous* "denotes, speaking generally, the seat of reflective consciousness, comprising the faculties of perception and understanding, and those of feeling, judging and determining."[2]

Throughout this study, I've basically put the teachings from week to week in order of the lyrics. Initially I had "Open Your Eyes" as day one but I moved it to day two. Why? Because you have to let God into your heart and your life first before you can have your eyes opened to see spiritual truths. Up until the time that you surrender your life to Christ, you will have distorted vision. Your thoughts, purpose, perceptions, understanding, judging and determining will be corrupted. And you won't even know it.

Pray about that today. If today is the day that you decide to let Jesus in the door of your life, I rejoice with you as do all of the angels in heaven (Luke 15:10). If you have been walking with the Lord for some time, ask God to show you areas and issues that you need to work on so that your vision aligns with His. Pray for those around you that don't know the truth of Jesus Christ and are not ready to admit that they are sinners in need of a Savior. Pray that the their minds would no longer be blinded. If you are in a group study, pray for the other participants as they come to mind. Ask God to give you 20/20 vision.

☼ Pray over what you have just studied and learned. Ask God to help you retain what you need to for real transformation in your life. Pray also for the requests that you have on your *Prayer Pages* in the back of this book.

Day Three: Bring Him Every Broken Part (the wounds and scars)

As I mentioned in the opening video this week, I had a four-pound mass removed that was cancerous. I have a scar from stem to sternum. It's a doozy. Unless I get plastic surgery, I will always have that scar. It will lighten up over time, but it won't disappear. Do you have any visible scars? What about invisible scars? The invisible scars are especially lethal because they are hard to see and pinpoint and even we forget that we have time, sometimes.

The songwriters offer up this great lyric in the bridge as they tell us to "bring Me (Him) every broken part, the wounds and scars of who you are." I hope that you have already brought your wounds and scars to Jesus so He could touch and heal them. And if you have, I hope that you've been able to tell others about your experience with our God who heals (Jehovah Rapha).

We run into trouble when we don't acknowledge hurt and pain. We press on with our lives and try to create as much distance as we can from the event or person. We delude ourselves into thinking that if we just "move on" that we'll get past the hurt and our lives will be better. But then…those moments and memories rush back and cloud our judgement, trigger an unhealthy reaction or just flat out depress us…and we're back to the pain.

We can't live like that and be healthy people. We have to bring our hurts, habits and hang-ups to the one who can heal us, strengthen us and make us wiser in the future. When we just sit with God – we sit in His presence – and we tell Him what we are struggling with, what we feel, what we need; He will give us His peace and, over time, we start the healing process. Bit by bit.

I always want to write Bible studies that everyone can relate to. Maybe this is not an area that you need help in. You routinely take time to meet with the Lord and you don't have any old hurts stored up. If so, that's great. But guess what? Someone that you know needs prayer. Someone is stuck with a big hurt that they can't get past and your prayer is going to help them clear that hurdle. God might even bring someone to mind that you need to pick up the phone and call. God could ask you to be vulnerable by sharing your story (aka testimony) of how He helped you heal and grow in your faith. When you do any of those things – pray, call, share – that will be your worship and that will please God.

> Wounds turn into scars, scars turn into testimonies,
> testimonies help people to see the work of God today.
>
> – Sach Conradie's YouTube comment on Mandisa's song "What Scars are For"

☿ Pray over what you have just studied and learned. Ask God to help you retain what you need to for real transformation in your life. Pray also for the requests that you have on your *Prayer Pages* in the back of this book.

Day Four: Hide "in Him" not from Him

A huge lesson that I learned about trust some years ago, (thank you Chaplain Shirey), was that we are to trust in God and God alone. Not people. Nowhere in the Bible does it say we are to trust in people. That took me a bit to wrap my mind around. It bears repeating. Nowhere in the Bible does it say to trust in someone other than God. By contrast we are told many times over to trust in the Lord.

Stop and let your brain process that for a minute.

We set ourselves up for disappointment and failure when we put our trust in people. People will undoubtedly let us down and, when they do, we are to love and forgive them anyway…but not trust them, because only one person is worthy of our trust, and our worship. God. He and He alone is worthy of our trust…and our worship.

Hiding. It all started in the garden of Eden and that didn't end well for Adam or Eve. It's human nature to want to hide the parts of us that we are embarrassed about. It just is. When you meet someone, you want to put your best foot forward. You don't open a conversation by stating your faults, failures and flops, that is unless you are going to an Alcoholics Anonymous (AA) meeting. Maybe that is why AA has stood the test of time. I had another wise person (thank you Chaplain Armstrong) point out that the church should be more honest like AA is. Another piece of truth that made me think deeper.

While there is wisdom in not sharing every detail about yourself with just anyone, God can be trusted with it all. Every. Single. Detail. He wants you to know, deep down, that He already sees your brokenness, wounds and scars. He already knows your "stuff." He is a safe friend (remember that from lesson four). He is a refuge. Our hiding place.

Read and write out the following scriptures:

Psalm 32:7

Psalm 57:1b - I will hide...

Psalm 62:8

Take time to do a personal inventory and ask yourself if there is any part of you that you have not trusted to Him or handed over to Him. Do you put your trust into other people or things besides God (i.e. your job, your spouse, your savings account, etc.)? How can you trust God and lean into Him more as your refuge?

 Pray over what you have just studied and learned. Ask God to help you retain what you need to for real transformation in your life. Pray also for the requests that you have on your *Prayer Pages* in the back of this book.

Day Five: Weekly Finale

Some of the learning objectives that we have covered this week were to:

- El Roi is translated as "the God who sees me."

- Some people have eyes and ears but they cannot see or hear. They are spiritually blind.

- Letting Him in means to surrender, obey & submit.

- God is our hiding place, refuge and safety. (Psalm 32:7)

- All things are open and laid bare before God. (Hebrews 4:13)

- The god of this world, Satan, has blinded the minds of the unbelieving. (2 Corinthians 4:4)

- Hide "in Him" not from Him.

Take time today to review all of your work from this week: the group lesson, your daily studies. Finish up anything that may be left undone. Spend time on areas that you would like to focus on more.

- Pray over what you have just studied and learned. Ask God to help you retain what you need to for real transformation in your life. Pray also for the requests that you have on your *Prayer Pages* in the back of this book.

Session 6

Finale Celebration

DATE: _____

TIME: _____

My Contribution: _____

Shout joyfully to the LORD, all the earth. Serve the LORD with gladness; Come before Him with joyful singing.

Know that the LORD Himself is God; It is He who has made us, and not we ourselves; We are His people and the sheep of His pasture. -Psalm 100:1-3

Bible Study Leader: See website for the Finale Celebration Planning Guide
www.worshipquest.com

Notes

Session One

[1] Donald S. Whitney, *Spiritual Disciplines for the Christian Life*, (Colorado Springs, CO: Nav Press 1991), 87.

[2] W.E. Vine, Merrill Unger and William White Jr., *Vine's Complete Expository Dictionary*, (Nashville: Thomas Nelson, 1996) s.v. worship.

[3] John Piper, Quoted in Ron Man, "Worship and the Glory of God," *Reformation and Revival Volume 9*, 2 (Carol Stream, IL: Reformation and Revival Ministries, 2000), 81.

[4] William Temple, Quoted in Kenneth O Gangel, "Reexamining Biblical Worship" *Bibliotheca Sacra Volume 142*, 566 (Dallas, TX: Dallas Theological Seminary, 1985), 165.

[5] Delesslyn A. Kennebrew, "*What is True Worship?*" accessed on March 23, 2019, https://www.christianitytoday.com/biblestudies/bible-answers/spirituallife/what-is-true-worship.html.

[6] Matthew Henry, "*Commentary on Psalms 90*," accessed on April 8, 2019, https://www.blueletterbible.org/Comm/mhc/Psa/Psa_090.cfm.

[7] Jason Soroski, "*What Does Selah Mean in the Bible and why is it important?*" accessed on January 12, 2020, https://www.crosswalk.com/faith/bible-study/what-does-selah-mean.html.

[8] Paul Enns, *The Moody Handbook of Theology* (Chicago, IL: Moody Publishers, 2008), 724.

Session Two

[1] Bob Kauflin, *Worship Matters*, (Wheaton, IL: Crossway Books 2008), 17.

[2] Ibid, 25.

[3] Ibid, 26.

[4] Ibid, rephrased, 26.

[5] James Strong, *The Strongest NASB Exhaustive Concordance*, (Grand Rapids, MI: Zondervan 2004), s.v. 4352 and 7812.

[6] "*Tear Bottle History,*" accessed on March 2, 2019, http://www.lachrymatory.com/History.htm.

[7] J. Vernon McGee, "*What is Worship?*" accessed on March 5, 2019, https://www.blueletterbible.org/Comm/mcgee_j_vernon/eBooks/what-is-worship.cfm.

[8] K. Eric Thoennes, *"How God is Both Incomprehensible and Knowable at the Same Time,"* May 25, 2016, accessed on March 12, 2019, https://www.crossway.org/articles/how-god-is-both-incomprehensible-and-knowable-at-the-same-time/

[9] Kauflin, *Worship Matters*, 25.

[10] Ibid, 25.

[11] James Strong, *The Strongest NASB Exhaustive Concordance*, s.v. 4352 and 7812.

Session Three

[1] James Strong, *The Strongest NASB Exhaustive Concordance*, s.v. 4352 and 7812.

[2] Ibid, s.v. 5647 and 5648.

[3] C. H. Spurgeon, Sermon #1311, Aug 27, 1876, accessed June 17, 2019, http://www.spurgeongems.org/vols22-24/chs1311.pdf.

[4] James Strong, *The Strongest NASB Exhaustive Concordance*, s.v. 5647 and 5648.

Session Four

[1] Billy Graham, "Answers," October 14, 2007, accessed on July 13, 2020, https://billygraham.org/answer/how-can-we-fear-god-and-also-love-him-at-the-same-time-isnt-that-a-contradiction/.

[2] Eric Thoennes, *"How to Have a Healthy Fear of God,"* July 23, 2019, accessed on August 1, 2020, https://www.thegospelcoalition.org/podcasts/tgc-podcast/healthy-fear-god/.

[3] Merriam Webster, accessed on August 1, 2020, https://www.merriam-webster.com/dictionary/obedient, s.v. obedient.

[4] Christian Assemblies International, *"1,050 New Testament Commands,"* accessed on August 5, 2020, https://www.abc.net.au/reslib/201407/r1308729_17984331.pdf.

Session Five

[1] James Strong, *The Strongest NASB Exhaustive Concordance*, s.v. 3540.

[2] W.E. Vine, Merrill Unger and William White Jr., *Vine's Complete Expository Dictionary*, (Nashville: Thomas Nelson, 1996) s.v. nous.

PRAYERS

PRAYERS

PRAYERS

PRASERS

PRAYERS

PRAYERS

_____

_____

_____

_____

_____

_____

_____

_____

_____

_____

_____

Writing Exercises

If you just plain write out the scriptures, you can absorb them more deeply and retain them better. Slowing down your mind so you can stay focused on a word, line or verse has tremendous benefits. It's considered to be meditation, which is an important spiritual discipline. You don't have to be an artist to benefit from these techniques.

Here are a few simple ways you can slow down and try a little word lettering:

- Write out words as you normally would but make one word larger.

- If you know how to write in cursive, combine both printing and cursive.

- Write out a word or sentence and go back and go over the down strokes (the parts of the letters that you start at the top and go down).

- Use other writing instruments like markers, colored pencils, gel pens, etc.

To view more examples of these Meditation Moments,

click on the "writing" tab at www.worshipquest.com

You can also upload your work in the "writing group" on the Worship Quest Facebook page or email it to me and I'll post it for you.

VIRTUAL WORKSHOPS
where you live and learn.

Let's Zoom for one session or six.
We can focus on the song from my book
or one that you choose.

Customized Distance Learning - All Group Sizes

For more detailed info:
info@worshipquest.com

Continue the Quest

I hope that you have been inspired to continue your own personal Worship Quest, to be in the Word, to enlarge your worship and to grow closer to God.

I would love to hear from you and know what your Worship Quest experience was like. Consider sharing pictures or video from your highlight moments, your personal definition, or a definition by someone else that inspires your worship. If you have a song that you've been impacted by, I'd love to hear the back story. Whatever it is, you can email me at info@worshipquest.com.

More Worship Quest Bible studies are in progress. Follow us on our Social Media and subscribe on the website to receive updates and announcements as the Worship Quest experience develops.

     www.worshipquest.com

Thank You

To my family, especially my husband David, who heard time and time again, "sorry honey, I have to work on the book."

To my friends who prayed for me, sent me little notes at just the right time and told me not to give up when the work became overwhelming.

To my test pilot group. Thank you for taking the time to do the study and then giving me honest feedback.

To my creative team who served as inspiration and advisors along the way:

- My informal editing team, Pat Davis and Dr. Lynn McCallister
- Michelle Peng for designing the book cover that served as brand inspiration
- Carly Norwood for serving as my informal creative director and helping me make critical corrections when it came to video production
- Lary Holland for web construction (bumpyroadstudios.com)
- James Armstrong for telling me the truth when it came to my own designs and turning me on to more competent production resources

As I went to upload this book to print, I had one last grammar question to solve so I went back to my high school English teacher, Ann Reasner. Thank you to all my English and Journalism teachers who equipped me to be here. Your tireless work pays dividends. Overlook my errors!

To self-publishers everywhere, there's never been a better time to share what God puts on your heart. May you be encouraged to take your next step of faith.

Lastly and most importantly, to the Lord Himself, who reached my heart through music and has entrusted me with this important message. I will never be able to thank you and worship you enough for all you have done for me, but I will try my very best.

WOR HIP
QUE T

About the Author

Christine (Chris) Young loves and lives in the great Mitten State with her husband David and their fur babies. After marrying her husband, she temporarily left her home state to become a military spouse and mother to a boy and girl, now full-grown adults.

Prior to returning to Michigan in 2014, she spent over a decade traveling and training women's ministry leaders in various countries. A professional vocalist since age fourteen, she is also a Bible study teacher, worship leader speedy Chevy Corvair driver and loyal Coca-Cola customer.

Chris holds an M.A. in Christian Ministry (Leadership) from Liberty Seminary, a B.S. in Public Relations and an A.A.S. in Marketing.

For more detailed author information
click on the "About" tab at
www.worshipquest.com

Made in the USA
Monee, IL
05 February 2021